I MUST STAND GUARD OVER MY HOME

VANSHIKA KHAITAN

EDITED BY
MEENA KANDASWAMY

Copyright © 2024 Vanshika Khaitan

All Rights Reserved.

This book has been self-published with all reasonable efforts taken to make the material error-free by the author. No part of this book shall be used, reproduced in any manner whatsoever without written permission from the author, except in the case of brief quotations embodied in critical articles and reviews.

The Author of this book is solely responsible and liable for its content including but not limited to the views, representations, descriptions, statements, information, opinions and references ["Content"]. The Content of this book shall not constitute or be construed or deemed to reflect the opinion or expression of the Publisher or Editor. Neither the Publisher nor Editor endorse or approve the Content of this book or guarantee the reliability, accuracy or completeness of the Content published herein and do not make any representations or warranties of any kind, express or implied, including but not limited to the implied warranties of merchantability, fitness for a particular purpose. The Publisher and Editor shall not be liable whatsoever for any errors, omissions, whether such errors or omissions result from negligence, accident, or any other cause or claims for loss or damages of any kind, including without limitation, indirect or consequential loss or damage arising out of use, inability to use, or about the reliability, accuracy or sufficiency of the information contained in this book.

Made with ❤ on the Notion Press Platform
www.notionpress.com

To the guardians of roots and rivers,
To those whose voices echo through the valleys,
And to the silent strength of those who remain unseen
This book is for you,
For the home you stand guard over.

Table of Contents

PREFACE

This book is a vigil, a call to stand guard over voices often silenced, their stories washed away like traces in river mud. The pages speak for those whose voices often go unheard, whose stories speak of the very soul of Jharkhand.

Anuj Lugun and Jacinta Kerketta bear witness through their poems, weaving verses that are anything but silent. These poems don't just describe a world; they embody it. They hold the weight of survival, the endurance of people whose very existence is an act of rebellion. To translate these words is to honour that defiance, to carry their truth into a language that reaches beyond borders. This isn't just poetry; it's a rhyme of lives entwined with the land, lives that refuse to fade into oblivion.

So take these pages slowly. Let each page linger. Let each word remind you of what endures beyond loss. Let these poems stay with you, stirring an awareness of the worlds we too often pass by. This book is Jharkhand's story, raw and unfiltered, inviting you to stand guard over a heritage that defies erasure.

EDITOR'S NOTE

It was a pleasure and a privilege to work on this chapbook featuring the works of two prominent radical Adivasi poets, Anuj Lugun and Jacinta Kerketta presented here in their English translation by Vanshika Khaitan. The choice of the two poets together in a single collection was a powerful choice to make; as we read their poems side by side, we can take in the full range of powerful critic and socio-political commentary offered by the poets.
Jacinta writes,

One day,
every girl from the forest
will write poetry.

How will you dismiss them?
What will you say, sir?

That it is not poetry,
but news?

These lines serve as an entry point into this anthology. Adivasi poets whose work highlights the tension between the corporate-militarised state using force to grab people's lands on the one hand and the indigenous marginalised communities fighting for their autonomy, survival and dignity on the other hand. Having to document this rupture, this slow annihilation of democratic behaviour from the ever-expanding state makes the poems appear like news. This urgency to chronicle struggles is a direct consequence of the mainstream media callously embracing state violence in the name of development and turning a blind eye to the people's resistance.

Anuj and Jacinta both show the profound connection between nature and how the fierce resistance against the forces threatening the Adivasi way of life is a collective attempt to preserve this planet. The poems are celebratory of the indigenous people's culture and identity just as they celebrate resistance and resilience. Their poems are bold assertions of the poet's right to speak truth, to challenge power, and the staunch opposition to be assimilated. For the marginalised, assimilation often becomes a euphemism for erasure (if not annihilation) —— and these poems stand testament to that nuance.

Meena Kandasamy
12 October 2024

INTRODUCTION

Anuj Lugun and Jacinta Kerketta are voices anchored in the soil, rivers, and skies of Jharkhand. They speak from a place that is unshakeable, a land as inseparable from their words as roots from earth. Their poetry is not for the faint-hearted; it's a witnessing of survival, each line insists, *"We are here. We belong."*

Anuj Lugun, often called the "Young Warrior Poet", brings a love for his homeland into every verse. In one of his interviews, he reflects on the power of his writing: *"My poetry is not just a creative outlet; it is a way to protect what is ours."* He is unafraid to confront exploitation and erasure, describing his work as a bridge between his people's inner worlds and the political landscapes they navigate. Anuj's words are rooted in the daily lives of his community, the scars of lost lands and threatened culture. His lines reflect a yearning for justice and echoes the essence of ancestral memory: *"To write is to remember, to remember is to resist."*

Jacinta Kerketta, a poet and journalist, speaks from a place of faith in her culture's resilience. She calls her poetry *"a language of survival"*, a language she has always known even if it remained unnamed for years. "*When I write*", she shares in an interview, "*I feel like I'm sitting on the ground, in the village, listening to the voices of my people echo across generations*". Her poetry is tactile, capturing the scent of wet earth, the rhythm of folk songs, and the ache of displacement. Jacinta's words are unadorned yet piercing; she writes to bear witness, to make visible the invisible. In her own words, *"I write because silence has been forced upon us for too long."*

Their poetry is both mirror and map, reflecting the resilience of a world they refuse to let fade, mapping a way forward even as they honour what remains. In Anuj's voice, you hear the rebellion, the longing for a land unscarred. In Jacinta's, you find the whispered hymns of a culture's unbroken spirit, resilient despite centuries of upheaval.

Together, their words are as much Jharkhand as the rivers that carve its valleys and the forests that blanket its hills. Their poetry belongs to a world where land and language are kin, where every phrase is rooted in a landscape that breathes through them. To read these poems is to enter a world held together by those who have stood guard over it, who continue to sing its stories even when no one is listening.

Our Funeral Pyre Cannot Be Royal

Anuj Lugun

In our dreams,
there has always been
a pair of oxen ploughing the field,
keeping the honour of the land alive.
In our dreams,
there has been a house by the banks of the Koel,
where our dreams are greater than we are.
In our dreams,
there has been the touch of River Karo,
which strengthens the bond of our embrace.
In our dreams,
there has been a wedding, wild with the beats
of the Mandar and Nagada drums.
We never wished for an empire,
we never desired a coronation.
Our idea of royalty was merely
for a handful of dreams to come true—
for the tight clasp of arms in our last breath,
and the final deep seal of red lips.

We wished that
even if the pigeons' sleep was broken by the scurrying of squirrels,
their dreams would not shatter.
We wished that

the lineage of crops would survive,
along with the sky over the fields.
We wished for the forest to remain,
with its clans and tribes.
We wanted to see the earth as the earth,
a tree as a tree,
a river as a river,
the sea as the sea,
and a mountain as a mountain.
But between our desires and their fulfilment,
there lies a chasm,
as deep and wide
as the gap between Delhi and the Saranda forest,
as vast as the distance between Ranchi and Jaldega.
In this gulf stand—
children, determined to rise, but falling into garbage heaps;
women, raising questions against unwanted births;
farmers, peeling the cracks of their fields from their own skin;
and workers, melting iron in the furnaces,
fighting against their own decay.

To make their resolve burn hotter than fire,
to turn our wishes into reality
oh, my determined friend,
our funeral pyre cannot be royal.

At our death,
there will be no mourning melodies,
no pauses in life for grief.
Beyond the chatter of newspapers,
our funeral will have only a simple white sheet—
coloured with the hues of earth, sky,
air, water, and fire.
We will be remembered
only in the stories of those
who were wounded alongside us.
Whenever their tears fall,
the meaning of a royal funeral will fade.
People won't listen to their mourning songs;
they will only hear our stories.
At our final rites, songs of struggle will be composed.
In those songs, they will ask:
Why is the earth's colour like our skin?
Why is the sky smaller than our eyes?
Why does the wind move slower than our feet?
Why have we carved more paths than water?
Why is fire less intense than our words?

Oh, my battle-hardened friend!
You must never surrender.
We will die fighting,
on those wild paths,
at those crossroads,

on those riverbanks,
where life will be most possible.

The Guerrilla's Autobiography

Anuj Lugun

1.
I am in search
of a poem
that will uncover,
on the battlefield-
landmines, buried bombs,
and attackers in ambush.

Like a child
crying alongside
his dead parents
and loved ones,
for that poem
that will rescue him
from this hell.

2.
Is war fought
with planes, battleships, tanks,
and finally, with the signatures
of two heads of state?
I wonder—
if yes,
then in what kind of reality
are we living?

I speak to the media
and the journalist brothers.
They laugh, saying,
"It's my foolishness."

What could be more absurd than this:
The chickens from my yard are missing,
the pigs have vanished, even their pens.
The oxen that ploughed the fields
have either been swallowed by the land,
or the fields are buried under dung.
The river has changed its course,
flooding the village—or perhaps,
the entire village has sunk into the river.

I wander, searching for my kin,
while the newspapers receive ads
ten times more than before.
I will not write to any president;
he is not my friend,
nor does he know
the love story of my life.
To him, it would be just a joke
that I love my chickens,
the wild vines, fruits, and mountains.

I am in shock
over the sudden disappearance

of pigs, oxen, buffaloes,
and squirrels.
The president will view these separately.
He will divide the life of a cow,
and it will become a cause for violence.
He will speak of the 'Ganges,'
and the other rivers will rot.
He will split apart squirrels, wild buffaloes,
elephants, and us,
to offer his definition of life,
while we only wish to create
a better world with them.
He will laugh at such a letter,
saying,
our world is a dark, primitive place.

I call upon my kin and companions
to meet me in the forest
on the day of the heads of state summit.
I tell them there is no more forest,
river, mountain, or land
to retreat to—
no running to peck grains
in another corner
while one part burns.
Our children, our sisters,
our elders, our women

burn every day
in that same fire,
against the brutal, primitive pacts of modernity.

3.
Every day, someone pushes us
toward the battlefield.
We become ready
to fight the very ones
who shove us into war.

They say we are waging war.
We know
we are holding ourselves back
from entering it.

4.
A bird passes through the forest paths,
and somewhere there,
lies an enchanted tunnel.
The poachers,
following its footprints,
reach its village.
And until
that village is burned down,
the enchanted tunnel
is not a landmine.

5.
The poachers ask my old mother
the whereabouts of my forest.
My mother asks them back,
"Can your guns
kill a bird?"
They say, "Yes."
So, my mother replies,
she knows nothing.

6.
One day, a bird
came to me and asked,
"With a gun on your shoulder,
wandering night and day,
hungry and thirsty
along the wild paths—
do you find joy in this,
as I do
when I sing my songs?"

I gave her a faint smile,
and said,
"I am singing your song."

7.
I sit like this,
alone,

on the doorstep
in the twilight.
Everyone is returning
to their homes.
The hen, with her chicks,
has just entered the coop.
The oxen and goats,
chewing their cud,
have settled into their spots.
The pigs are lazily grunting,
exhausted.
I, too, have just returned from the fields.

Here, deep in the forest,
everything is still—
except for the night,
which continues its restless march.
The ancestors once cowered in fear,
mistaking it for a black demon,
but now, a freight train just passed through
this tribal village,
blaring its horn as it carried iron scrap,
and the procession will continue through the night...

The distinction between time and night
no longer exists,
as it once did when,

in the second watch of the night,
under the moonlight,
herds of elephants
and wild buffalo grazed.
In those days,
the moon did not arrive
as a mere postponement of the night.

We know the moonlight
can hold off the darkness
for a short while,
but the sun
is the final solution to end the night.
Knowing this,
waiting for its rise
is like shackling ourselves.
As I break these chains,
I wonder—
Do the oxen and goats,
chewing their cud,
know our grief?
Do they realise
that we are passing through
the same crisis?
After being evicted from this village,
there will be no pasture left,
neither for them, nor for us.

What will happen to the wild buffaloes,
our totems...
Kerketta... Dhechuwa... Horl...?

A night's stay
or a flash of a digital camera
cannot capture
our photo with our fellow creatures.
The journalists and travel writers
must understand
that our languages
have their own unique meanings,
which they have failed to grasp,
even through translation.
Which bird was turned into a guerilla
by the goat's sorrow?
For a shared grief,
a joint action is needed.
This should be asked
of those journalists
who fix their cameras
on a single corpse,
claiming to expose the system's failures,
while arguing that partisanship and resistance in poetry
are meaningless, artificial,
and unnecessary.

Murder shakes the human soul the most,
and it is in the face of murder
that it has the strongest arguments.
We don't want such arguments,
despite knowing
that our kin and companions
have been killed by those very arguments.
Critics bring these same arguments
to decorate, polish, and present poetry..
How can I bring art, structure,
and beauty into my poem...?
Oh... how beautiful is our village,
our land—
our companions, our forests...
Ichha Bahha and Simbua Buru.

The night continues,
the darkness spreads.
The moon cannot hold off the night for long.
Our oxen, goats, and chickens
know that our sorrow is shared.
We grieve because
our wives and children were killed
in fake encounters,
but even more painful
is the fact that

this truth is not allowed to reach
the neighbouring village.

Our identity feels like that of a sailor
lost on an island.
The news spreads,
but like legal clauses,
it requires the confirmation
of judges,
whose paths are exhausting, winding,
and endless...
For generations,
we have circled around their courts...
And I sit down,
with the weariness of centuries,
on my doorstep.

Soon, my firefly companions will arrive,
and I will join them.
Oh my ancestors! These fireflies
are the living forms of your souls.
Look at me—
I gather the songs of coexistence
into my palm with these fireflies.

8.
I am surrounded
by death at every moment,

yet I continue to sing.
Seeing me sing,
death becomes confused.
It wonders—
should it target me,
or my song?

There, by the riverbank,
when death attacked us,
it stood stunned,
watching why we fought
with such courage,
and wondering why
it should not feel ashamed
of its actions.
It turned back,
pondering that,
if the fragrance of ripe paddy
was planted into this earth,
all the children would play in celebration,
and it would be freed
from setting up battlefronts in war.
This land would become
a green field for children's games.
That day, death heard this song from us
and returned with our questions.

We know our poetry doesn't sprout
from a desert of words,
nor do we advocate
building homes on sand dunes.
The 'Sasan Diri' standing with our ancestors
understands the essence of being alive.
The sal trees
know the joy of birth.
The oxen recognize the language
of farming days.
Here, by this rocky mound,
or by that riverbank,
we sit,
thinking of our land.
We love the innocence of our children,
and their babbling voices
love us in return.
We assure them
with our eyes,
about their songs, fireflies,
butterflies, and dreams.

How peaceful it is
here on this mound...
in the valley of the mountain,
by the riverbank,
as we share our songs,

we exist in harmony.
A vine, entwined around a tree,
lifts a squirrel onto its body
and offers it a ripe fruit.
The river carves this scene
into its heart.
And the mountain... doesn't it bow
to peer into the river's eyes,
to witness it all?
Oh! The butterfly rolling on the flowers,
Oh! Grandmother firefly,
look, a little bird
has just given birth to a child.
Shouldn't we sing a song for her?
The fireflies, butterflies, flowers, trees,
rivers, forests—
all the living beings know
that our lives grow together,
in this way.

Note:
'Sasan Diri' refers to the cultural heritage stones of the Mundas, erected in memory and honour of ancestors over their graves, symbolising ownership of the village land. It is said that during colonial times, when the Mundas were

asked for ownership papers of their villages, they carried these stones to the court in Kolkata.

In Waiting for the Woman, the Moon

Anuj Lugun

That night, lying on the ground with her children and husband,
She gazed up at the sky,
Fixing her eyes on it,
The sky was still, silent, and steeped in emptiness.
For a moment, she thought,
And then carefully, she adorned the sky with
Her bangles, earrings, bindi, and a touch of kohl,
She placed them gently upon its body,
And the sky, now dressed,
Became more beautiful than ever before.
In the depths of the night, as everything lay still,
The winds blew softly through the valley
Where her small village nestled between the low hills.
Amidst the calm,
She searched through the gentle breeze,
For something to cradle her children and husband.
Just then, the moon crept close to her,
And whispered:
"Listen! It's been over a thousand years,
I've risen and set the same way,
Moving through my phases,
Talking, eating, living—just as I am.
Your touch, your artistry,

Can make me more beautiful,
You can shape me anew."
The woman glanced at her sleeping children, her husband,
And replied:
"I've just returned from working the fields with my husband,
And I've only just put my children and husband to sleep.
They are resting now,
And I must stand guard over my home.
When I'm free,
I'll do the work you ask,
But for now, go away."
The moon, hearing her answer, quietly left,
Waiting for her to return.
Even today,
The moon waits for that woman.

Adivasi

Anuj Lugun

Those who live in luxury,
Who seek convenience,
Who demand reservations,
They call themselves Adivasi.
Those who chase after votes
Tell us, *you* are Adivasi.
Those who spread their faith,
Label us as wild, primitive Adivasi.
Those who, in their hearts, believe
They are the true, original inhabitants,
Call us forest dwellers—*Vanvasi*.
But those who walk silently,
Barefoot along untamed forest trails,
They never say, *we* are Adivasi.
They know how to heal themselves
With the wild herbs of the jungle.
They understand the shifting moods of weather
By watching the animals stir.
Every tree, every plant,
Every mountain and river,
Knows who *they* are.

Clouds

Anuj Lugun

Above my head, the sky stretches wide,
And where I stand,
I hear the sound of water flowing
From the edge of a field.
Where I stand,
This is my land.
I stand before a mountain,
Watching the clouds swirl around its peak.
Truly, it's a beautiful sight,
Worthy of a poem,
A poem for my beloved.
But again and again,
The sound of water flowing from the field's edge
Draws my attention.
I look at the field,
At the water slipping away from its boundary,
At the mountain,
And at the clouds swirling above it.
I feel, deeply,
That the sky stretches above me, too,
And clouds hover there as well.
I grip the earth firmly
Beneath my feet,
And forget about writing a poem

For my beloved.
In this moment,
I am in love with the mountain
That carries clouds upon its crown.

What Was My Connection?

Jacinta Kerketta

While looking at the trees cut down
for the wide roads in Jharkhand,

That mango tree
stood right here, by the roadside,
where I used to wait every day
to catch my bus.
While I waited,
it would tease me,
throw a mango my way.
As soon as I bit into it, delighted,
I'd grumble, "It's a bit sour."
It would laugh:
"You always sleep on the bus, don't you?
This is to wake you up.
Alright, I'll drop sweet ones now,
I promise!"
And before I knew it,
the bus would arrive.

That day,
I reached the roadside to catch the bus,
but it was gone.

For years,
that mango tree had been waiting for me,
right there—
where could it have gone?
The next day,
I read in the newspaper
about its death.

I wept bitterly that day,
as if someone from my family had died.
I couldn't sleep all night,
wondering,
how could they have cut it down?

The next day,
I rushed to the spot,
thinking I'd gather its scent
and plant it in my courtyard.
Its fragrance would grow,
and then,
every time I left home,
I'd carry its scent with me.
When I returned,
I'd find its fragrance
standing there,
waiting for me.

But my dreams shattered
when a whirlwind of dust
began mocking me.
I saw my mango tree's scent,
struggling,
entangled with the swirling dust.

I ran to the police station,
to file a report:
my companion has been murdered.
The station burst into laughter,
brandishing a baton,
"First, tell us,
what was the nature of your relationship?"

Since then,
I've been wandering from place to place,
trying to explain
what my relationship was with it.
But now,
there's no one left.
Everything has vanished.
All that remains
are long, wide roads,
stretching far and barren,
with endless swirling dust...

Sir! How Will You Dismiss It?

Jacinta Kerketta

Sir!

You give ornate interpretations
to the subjects veiled
that are draped around us.
But what will happen on the day
a girl from the forest,
arriving in the city,
writes all the truth in her poem?

That truth,
which you've hidden
beneath the covers of your books,
your vile language
spoken in gestures
after you leave the stage,
those truths of yours
that you think will fade
into some illusion with time.

Sir!

One day,
a girl from the forest
will strip your interpretations bare

with her truth,
and write in her poem
how the guards of your forest
have, under the guise of searches,
torn her clothes,
how your troops break into
their homes,
how children start holding
guns instead of sticks,
and how her heart is filled
with gunpowder.

Sir!

One day,
every girl from the forest
will write poetry.
How will you dismiss them?
What will you say, sir?

That it is not poetry,
but news?

The Death of Mother Tongue

Jacinta Kerketta

The mother tongue was imprisoned
in the mother's mouth,
and the children
grew up demanding its release.
The mother tongue did not die on its own,
it was killed,
but the mother could never realise this.
In the face of the possibilities
that promised dreams of food,
she clenched her teeth for her children,
and beneath those dreams of morsels,
the mother tongue was buried.
Even today, the mother believes
the death of the mother tongue
was an accident.

Concern

Jacinta Kerketta

Mother,
Why do you spend your whole day
wandering through the forest,
crossing mountains,
returning home late in the evening
just for a bundle of wood?
Mother says:
I roam the forest,
scale the mountains,
wander all day long
only for the dry, fallen wood.
I cannot bring myself
to cut down a living tree!

The National Anthem Plays

Jacinta Kerketta

Deep within my thoughts,
The national anthem begins to echo suddenly,
And I find myself standing still,
Alert, tense, locked into attention—
Not because of reverence,
But for the fear of being branded a traitor.
At that precise moment,
A swarm of termites burrows into me,
Mistaking my body for a mound of earth,
Eating away at my core, hollowing me out.
I feel their gnawing, but my voice is trapped,
My mouth shut, unable to scream—
Yet I stand, motionless, in the posture of attention.
Outside, countless voices of protest,
Wound tight like a spring,
Prepare to rise up,
To pour out into the streets—
But just then,
The anthem reverberates within their walls,
Like a haunting echo,
A sound that grips every soul with fear.
It's as if a deadly whisper
Had just swept across the nation,
As if a gun's cold barrel

Had pressed against the nape of every neck,
Commanding submission,
Ordering all to freeze in place—
To stand, without question,
Rigid, in forced allegiance.
The national anthem plays on,
And I stand—
Straight, unmoving—
While inside, the termites writhe and feast,
Devouring me silently from within.
They dance freely in my hollow shell,
Unafraid, untouched by the accusations of treason
That hang over me,
As I remain trapped,
In a ritual I no longer understand.

REFERENCES

Lugun, Anuj. हमारी अर्थी शाही हो नहीं सकती / अनुज लुगुन- कविता कोश, http://kavitakosh.org/kk/हमारी_अर्थी_शाही_हो_नहीं_सकती_/_अनुज_लुगुन

Lugun, Anuj. गुरिल्ले का आत्मकथन / अनुज लुगुन- कविता कोश, http://kavitakosh.org/kk/गुरिल्ले_का_आत्मकथन_/_अनुज_लुगुन

Lugun, Anuj. औरत की प्रतीक्षा में चाँद / अनुज लुगुन - कविता कोश, http://kavitakosh.org/kk/औरत_की_प्रतीक्षा_में_चाँद_/_अनुज_लुगुन .

Lugun, Anuj. "आदिवासी / अनुज लुगुन." आदिवासी / अनुज लुगुन - कविता कोश, http://kavitakosh.org/kk/आदिवासी_/_अनुज_लुगुन

Lugun, Anuj. "बादल / अनुज लुगुन." बादल / अनुज लुगुन - कविता कोश, kavitakosh.org/kk/बादल_/_अनुज_लुगुन .

Kerketta, Jacinta. "उससे मेरा संबंध क्या था?" *Hindwi*, www.hindwi.org/kavita/usse-mera-sambandh-kya-tha-jacinta-kerketta-kavita .

Kerketta, Jacinta. "साहेब! कैसे करोगे ख़ारिज?." *Hindwi*, www.hindwi.org/kavita/saheb-kaise-karoge-kharij-jacinta-kerketta-kavita? .

Kerketta, Jacinta. "मातृभाषा की मौत." *Hindwi*, www.hindwi.org/kavita/matribhasha-ki-maut-jacinta-kerketta-kavita .

Kerketta, Jacinta. "परवाह." *Hindwi*, www.hindwi.org/kavita/parwah-jacinta-kerketta-kavita? .

Kerketta, Jacinta. "राष्ट्रगान बज रहा है: हिन्दवी." *Hindwi*, www.hindwi.org/kavita/rashtrgan-baj-raha-hai-jacinta-kerketta-kavita? .

ABOUT THE AUTHOR

Vanshika Khaitan is a high school student who writes with a purpose: to capture the voices that slip through the cracks, to stand guard over stories that matter. Already the author of a published poetry anthology, she sees writing as more than expression; it's a duty, a means to amplify what often goes unheard. Her work is rooted in a fierce belief that words carry weight, that each line has the power to hold a world, and that even the quietest voices deserve to echo.

With each poem, Vanshika seeks to make the invisible visible, to create a space where memory, resilience, and identity converge. Her writing is both a promise and a testament—that stories, no matter how small, must be told and held close.

www.ingramcontent.com/pod-product-compliance
Lightning Source LLC
LaVergne TN
LVHW041257150826
845673LV00008B/2632
* 9 7 9 8 8 9 6 1 0 4 5 4 4 *